Birds

Coloring Book for Adults

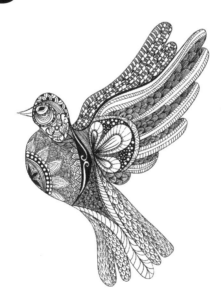

Yap Kee Chong
8345 NW 66 ST #B7885
Miami, FL 33166

Createspace

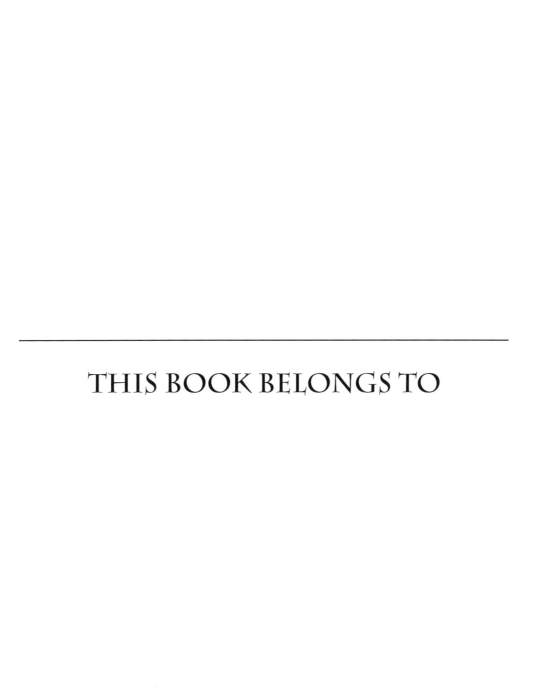

THIS BOOK BELONGS TO

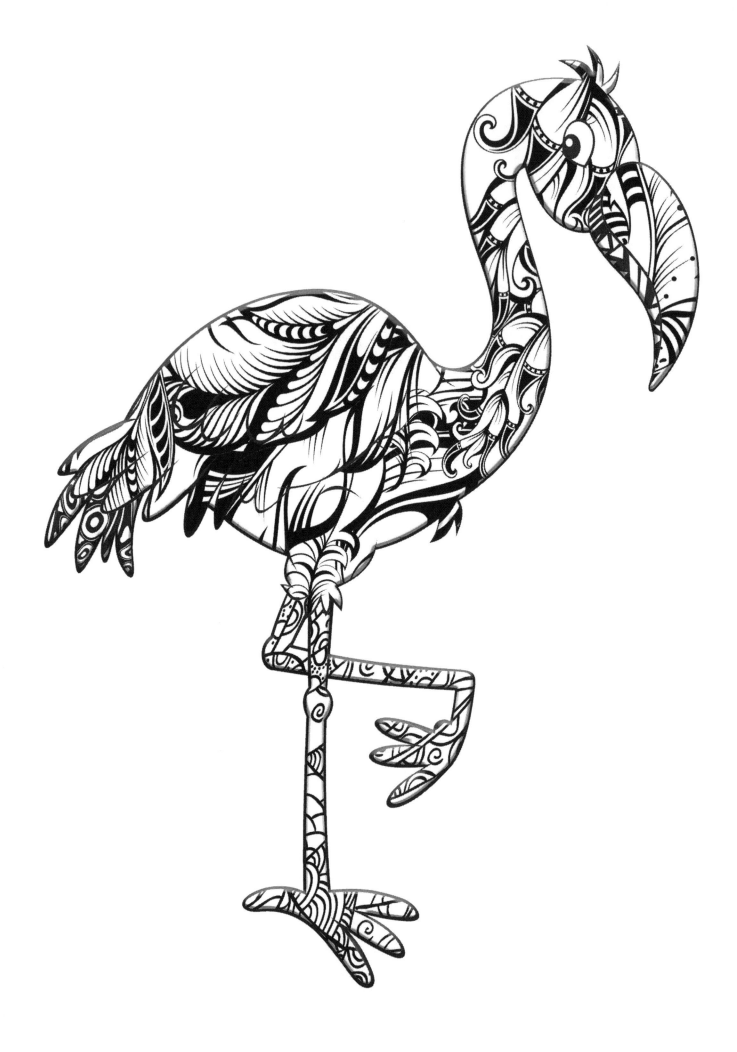

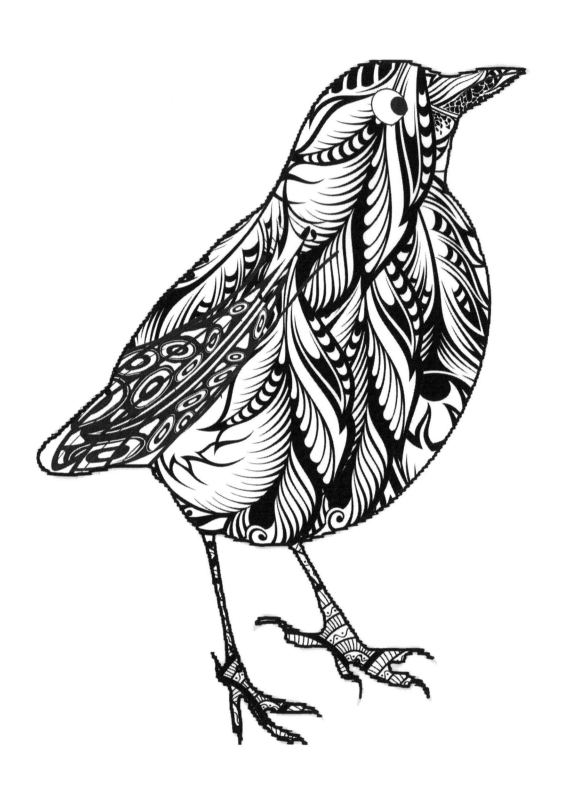

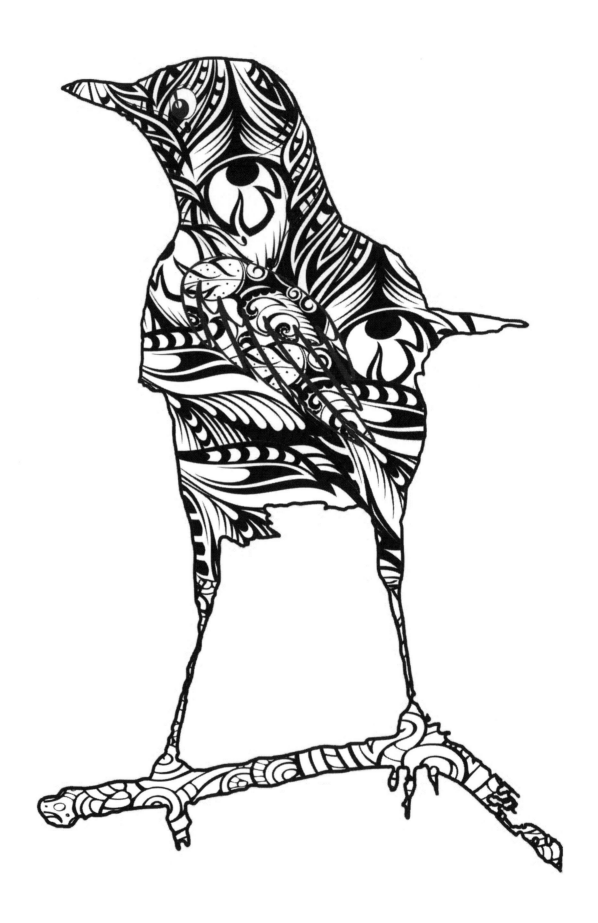

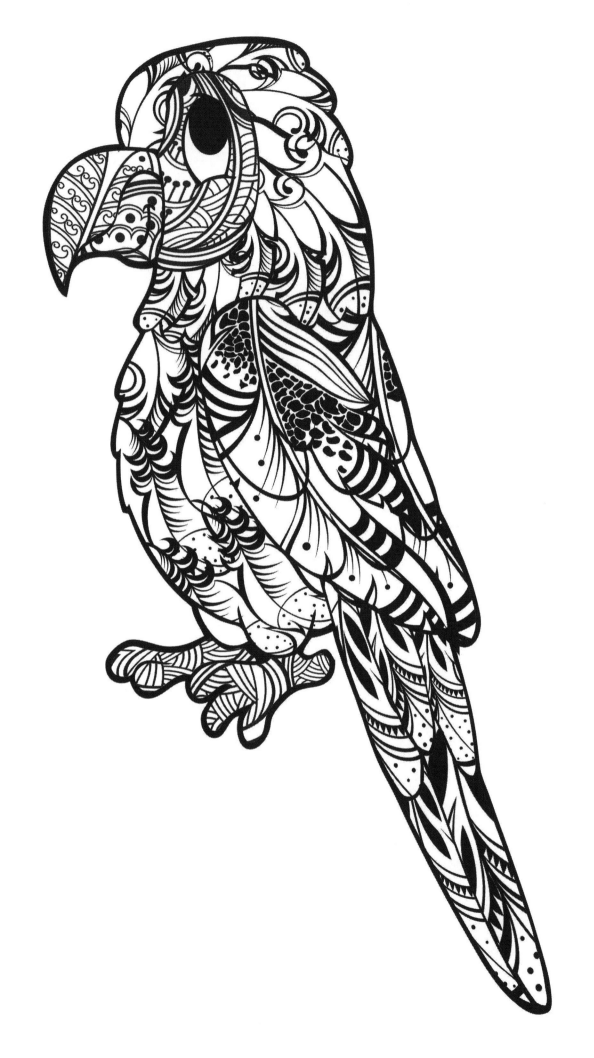

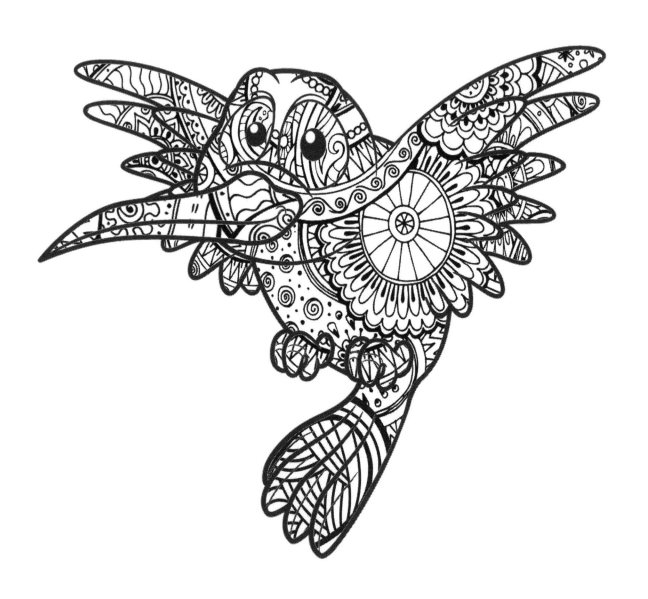

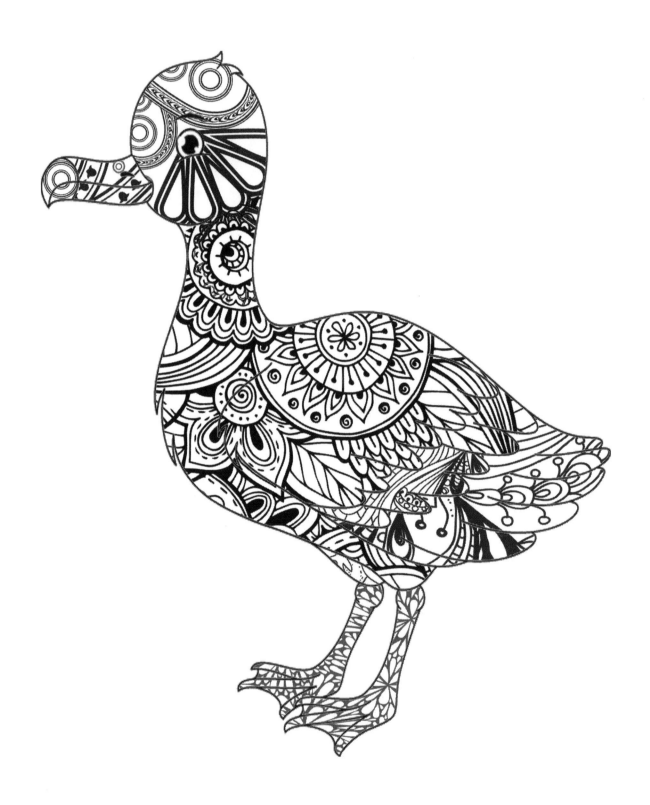

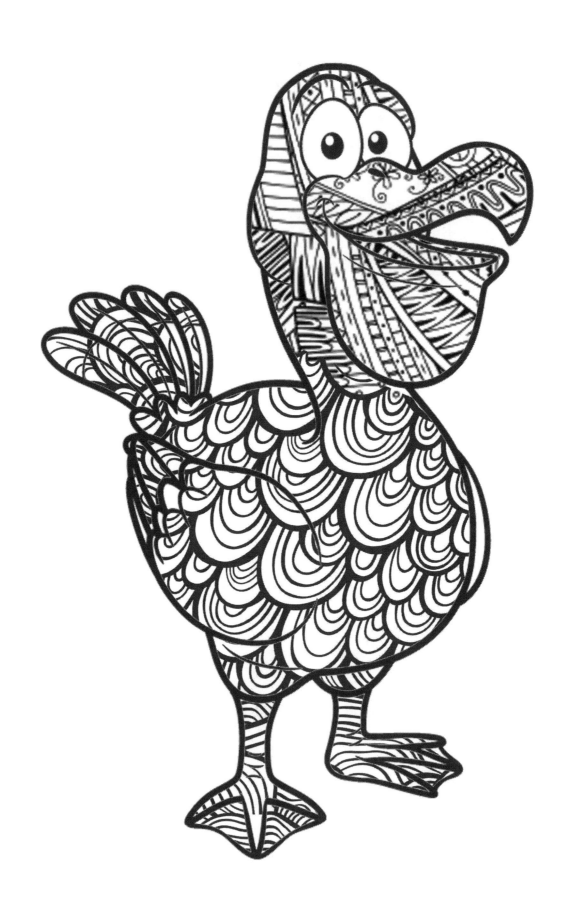

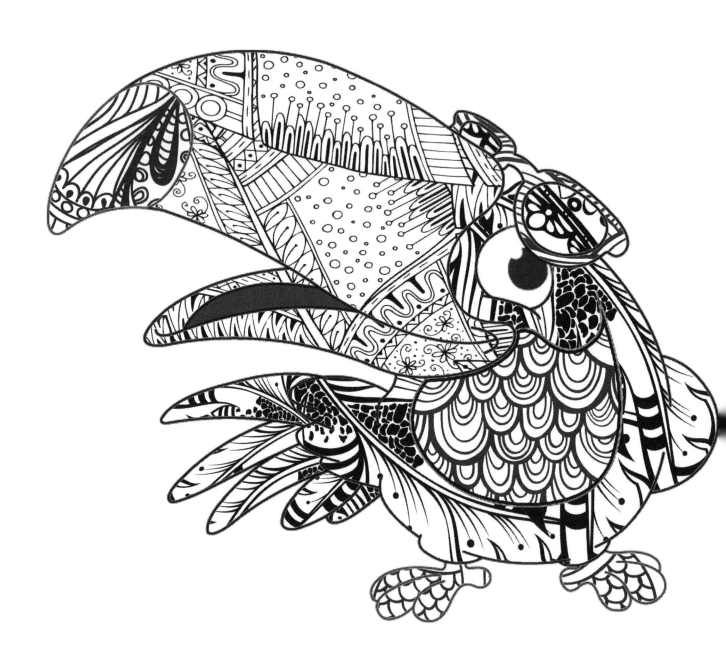

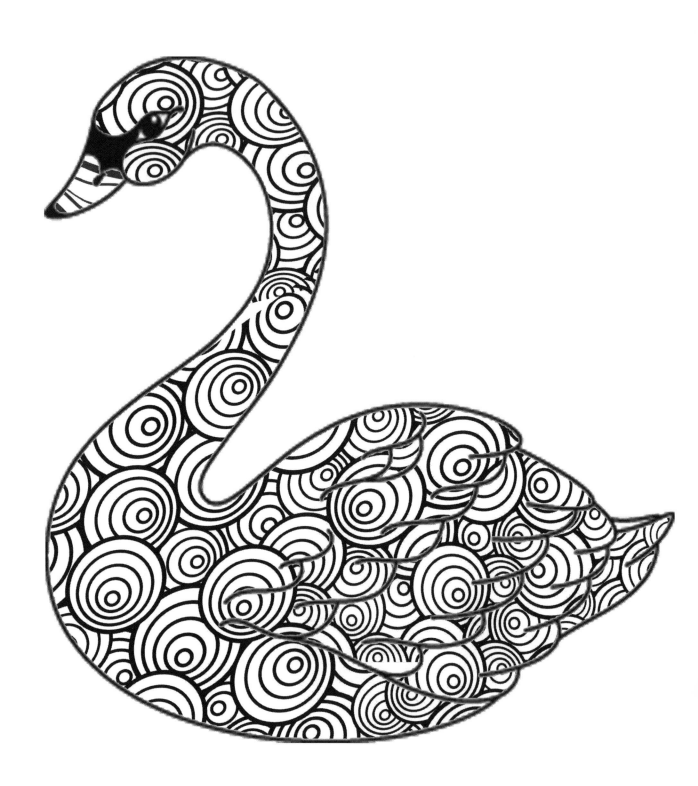

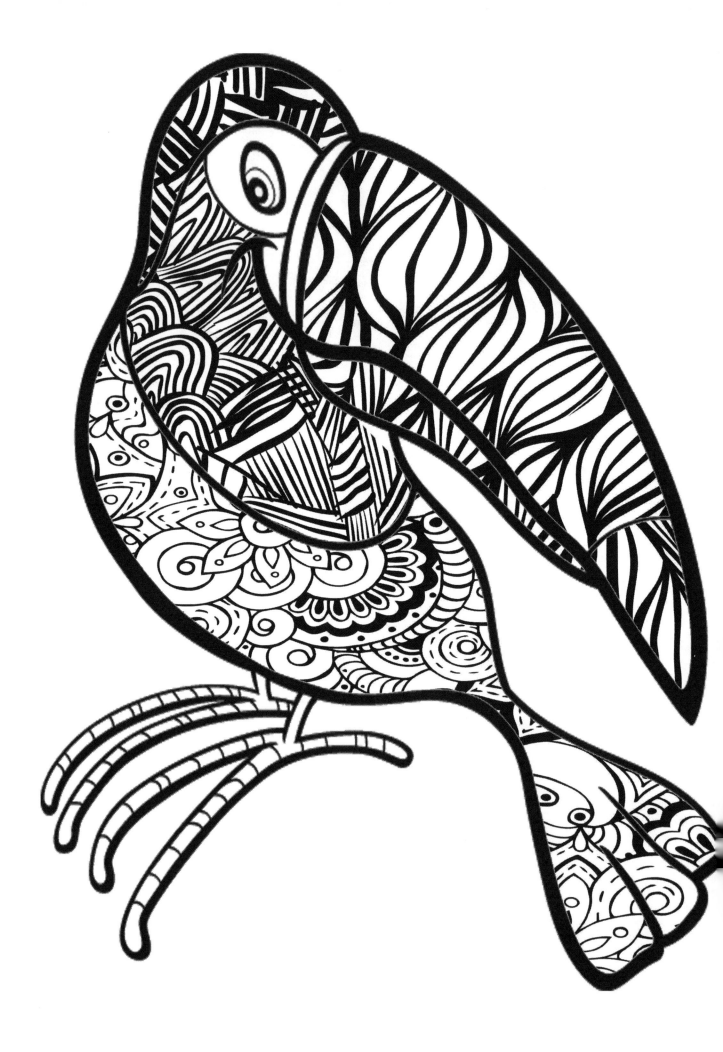

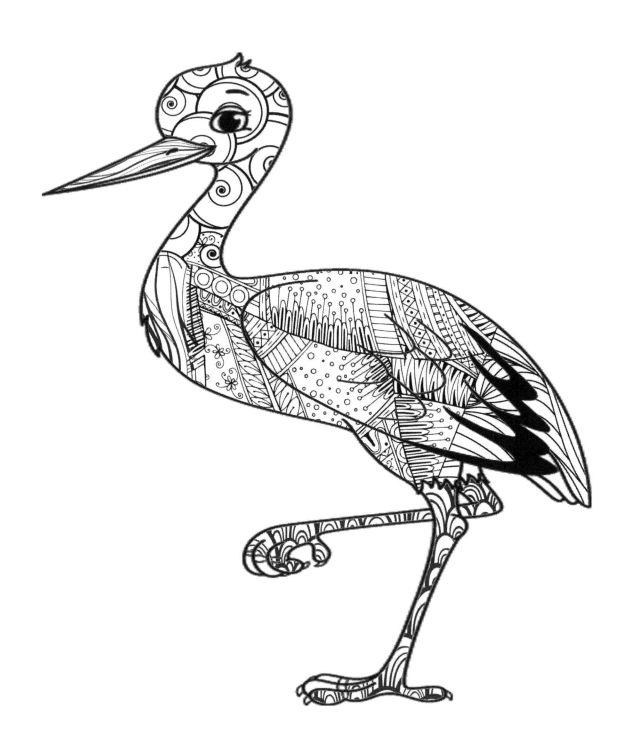

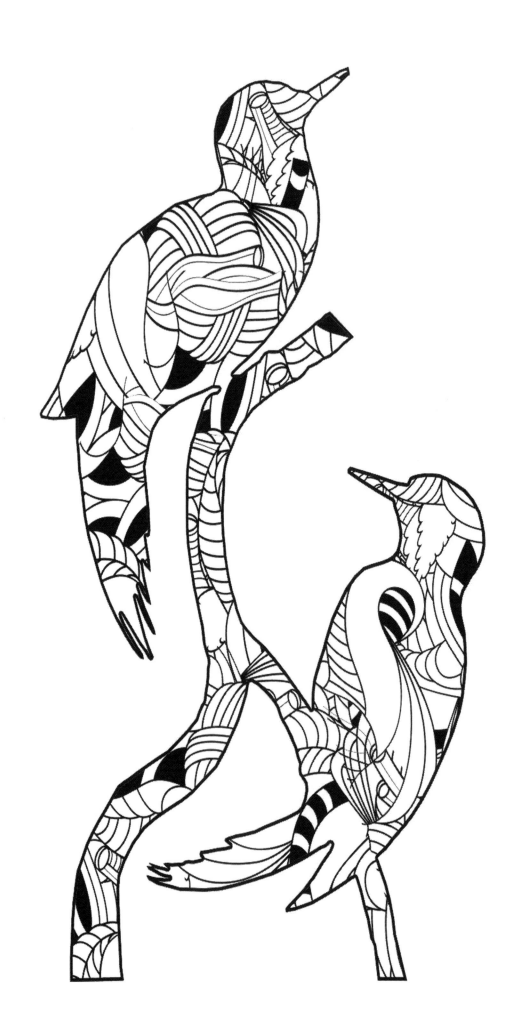

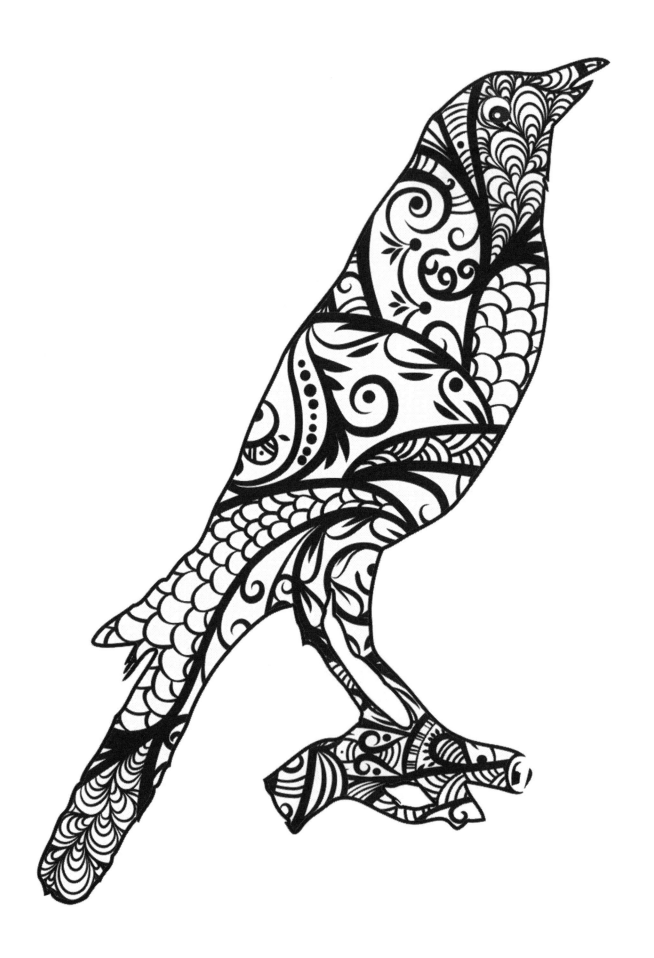

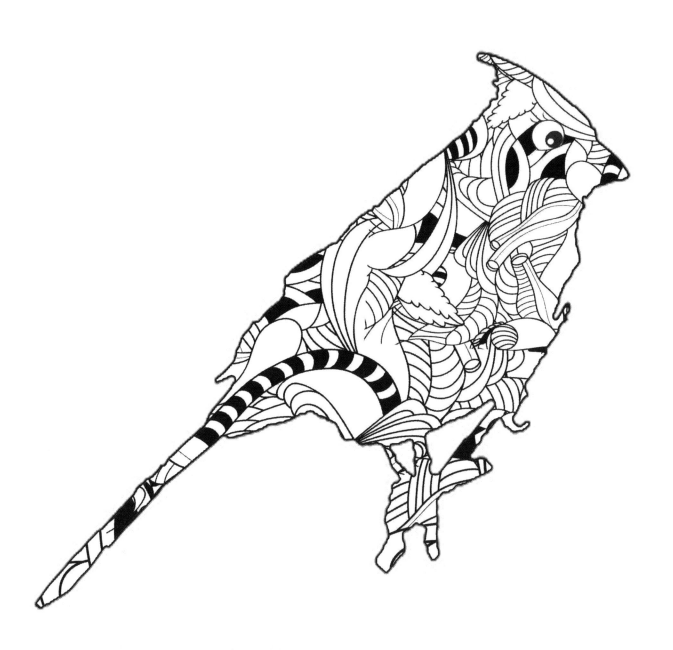

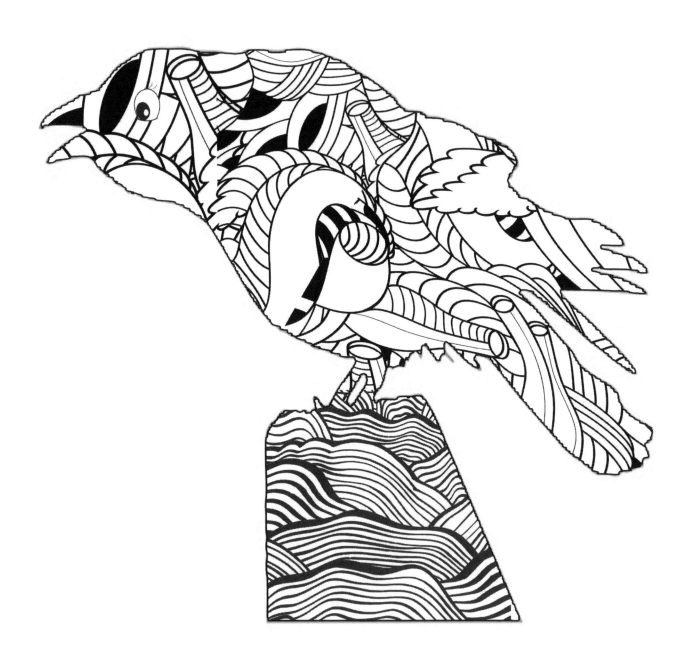

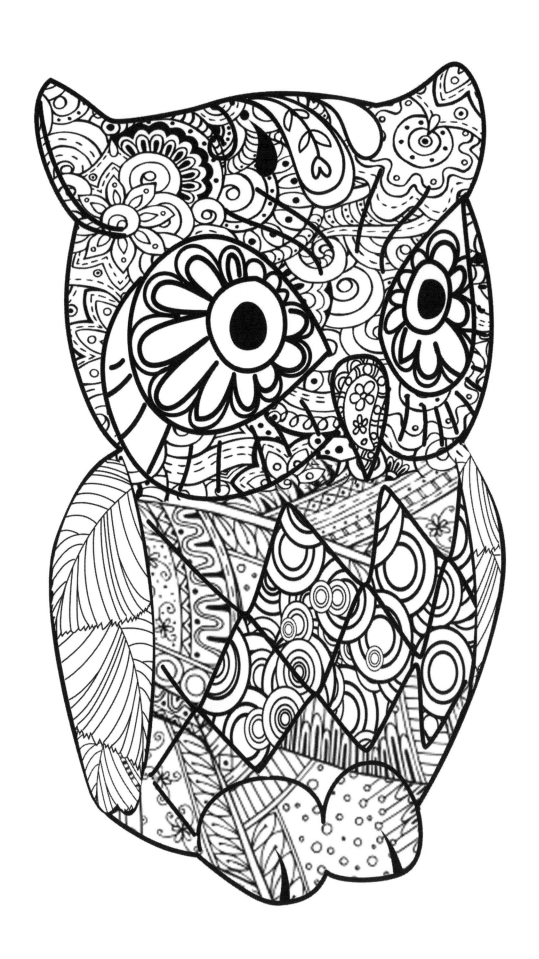

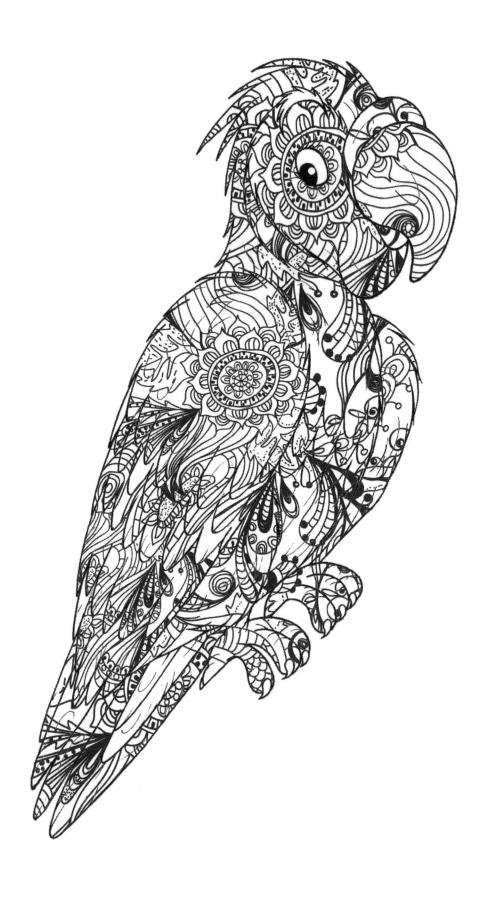

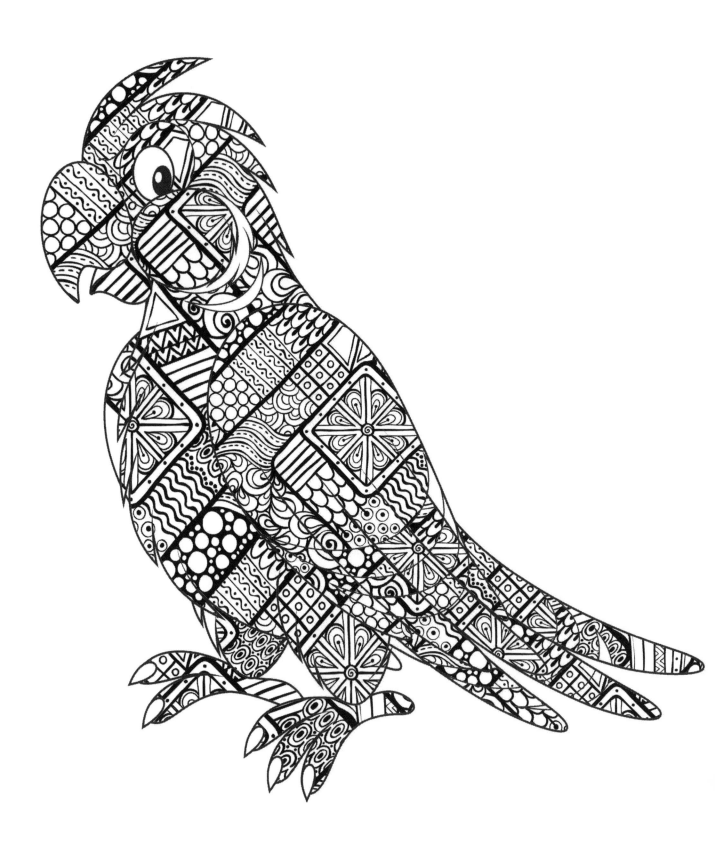

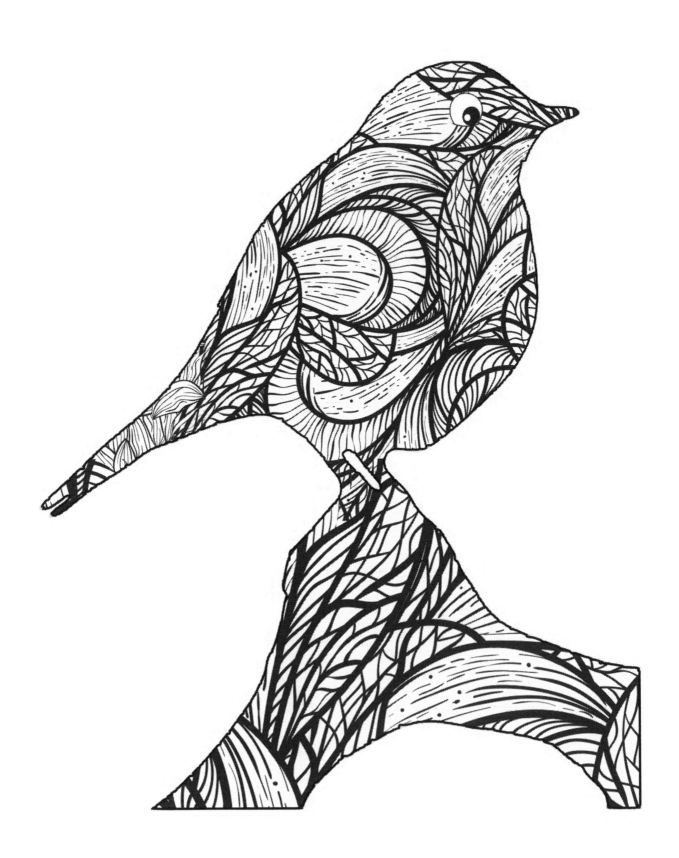

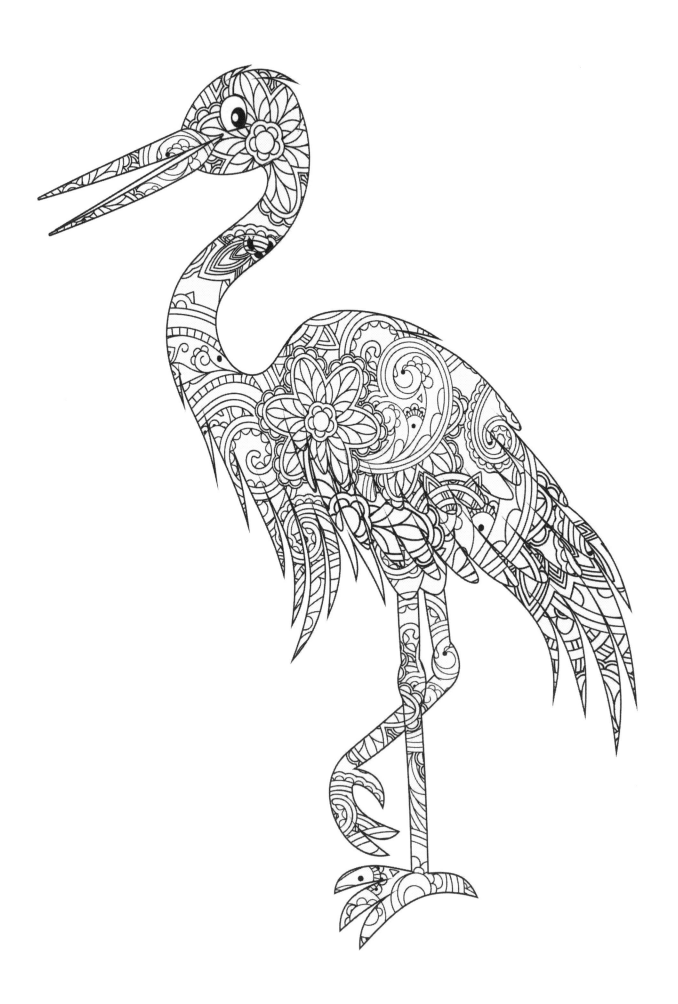

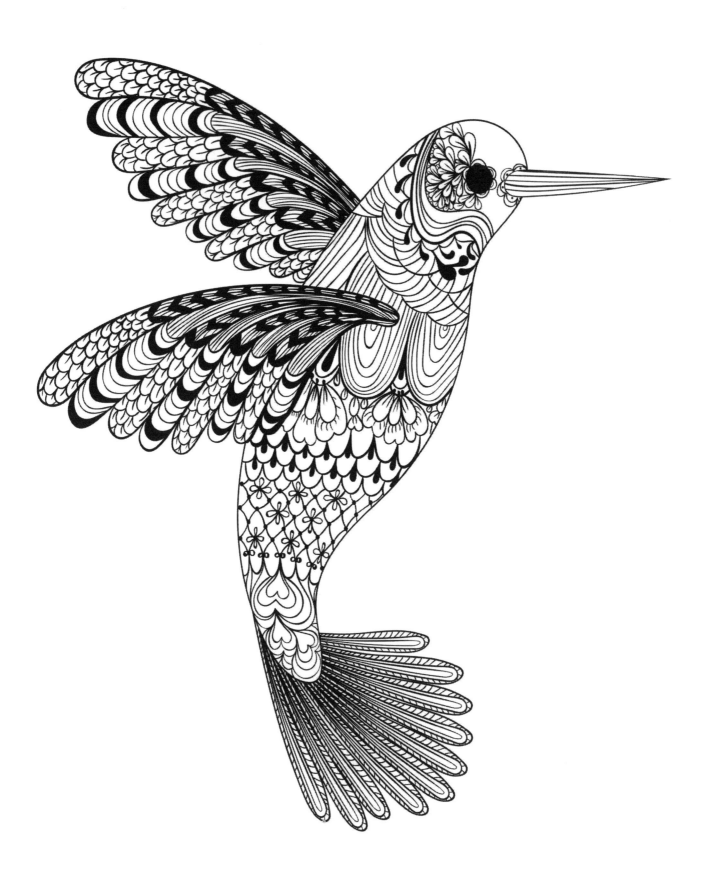

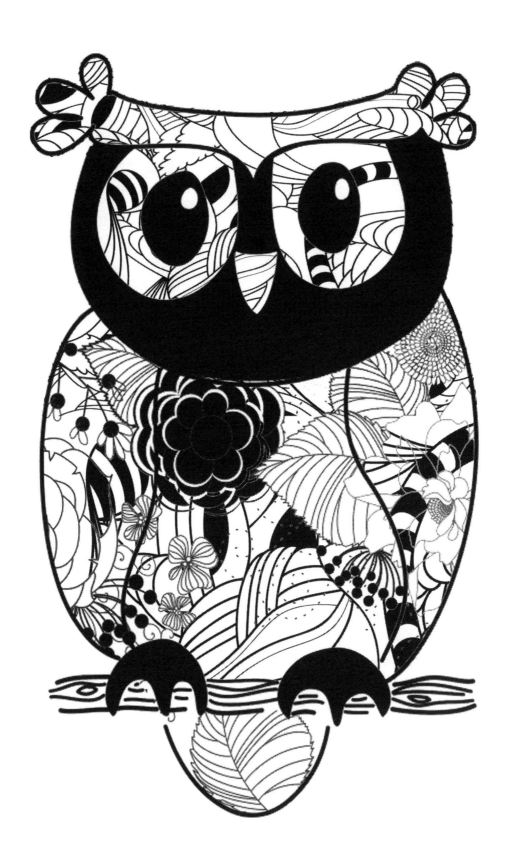

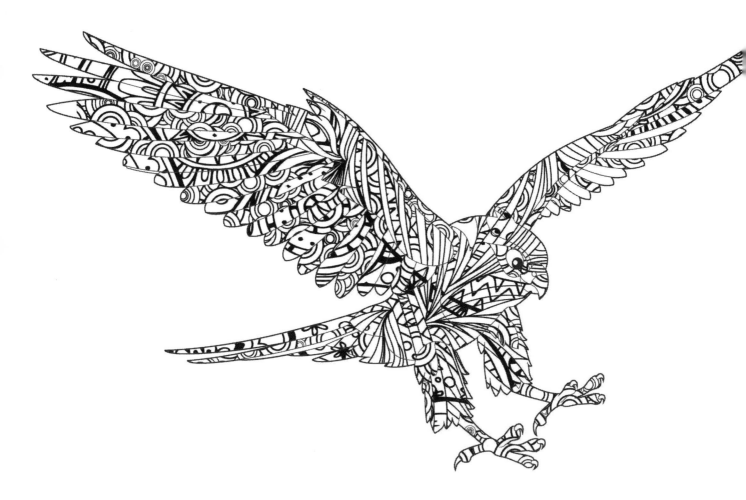

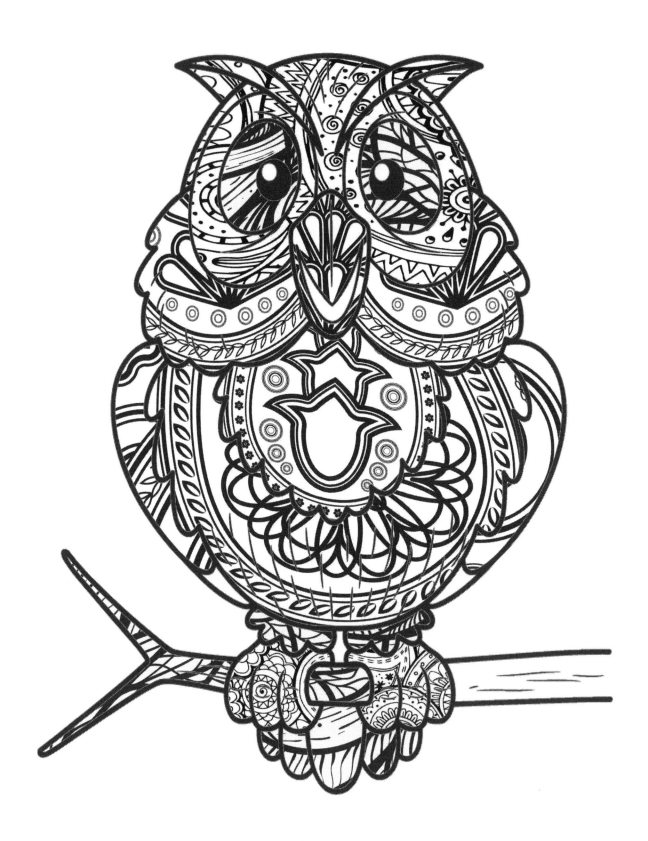

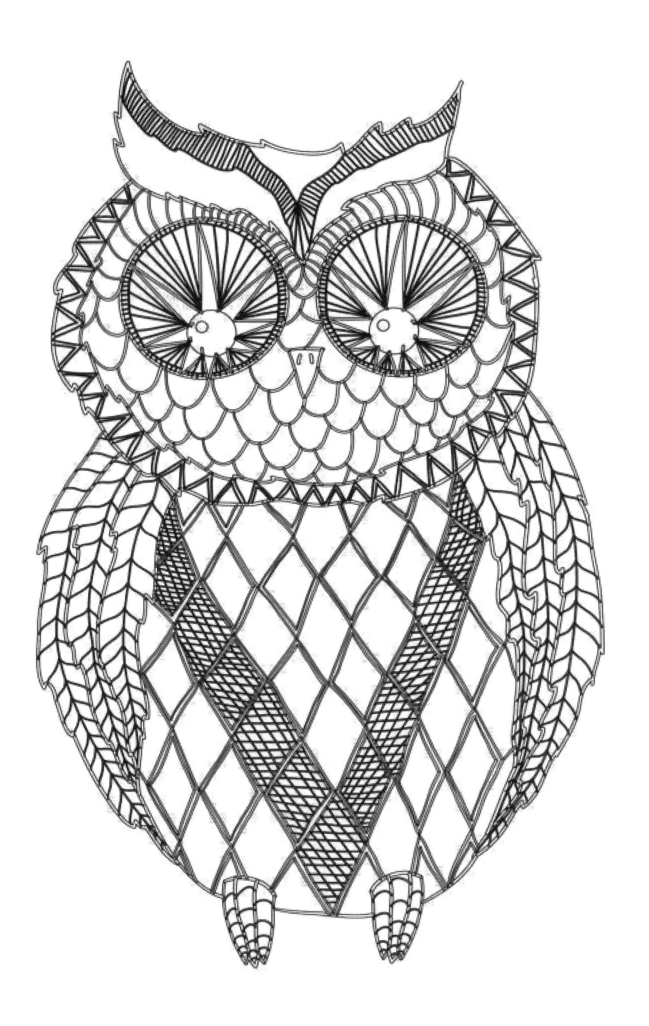

Check Out Our Other Coloring Books

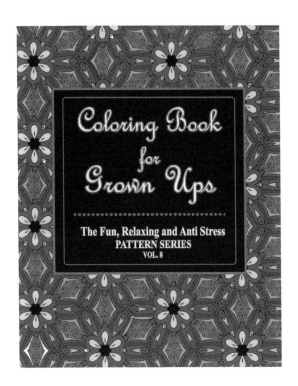

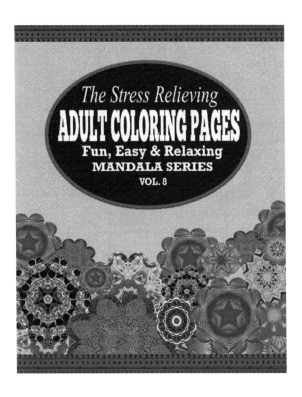

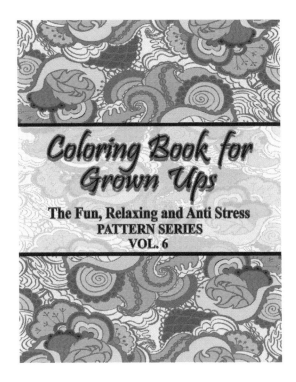

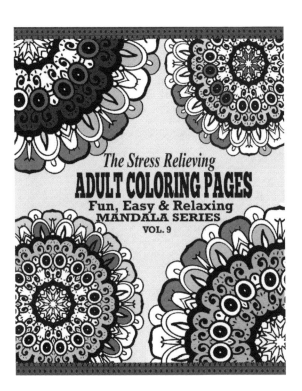

Made in United States
Troutdale, OR
12/10/2023

15617700R00031